Generational Curse Breaker's Fatigue

What No One Tells the Breaker

Markeida Faithe, LICSW

The Power Pusher

ISBN: 979-8-9857156-1-3

Dedication

This book is dedicated to all generational curse breakers who are confused about what their role truly means and requires. May this book serve as a catalyst to help you gain the necessary clarity and vitality to finish your race gracefully. May the words on each page equip you with the understanding and strategy needed to rise to the invitation of breaking your bloodline limitations. From my heart to yours, you will win if you faint not.

Markeida Faithe, The Power Pusher

Table Of Contents

Introduction

Hello, Generational Curse Breaker! Yes, I'm talking to you. I assume you chose this book not because you're trying to determine if you're a generational curse breaker, but because you know that you are. More than likely, the title caught your attention because it describes exactly where you find yourself on your journey: fatigued. Oh my! Bless your weary heart. I've been there a time or two myself, and just like you, no one told me that being called to such a prestigious role comes with challenges and requires wisdom to maneuver.

I'll let you in on a secret: if you're going to win the generational curse breaker's battle, you must possess knowledge and spiritual stamina. You can't win unequipped and worn out. To assist you, I wrote this book to help guide you to a place of inspiration where you become eager to get back into the fight. However, this time, you'll be much more prepared to face the challenges that generational curse breakers attract. Let's go!

Please be clear. This book is not written to teach you how to break curses. There are a trillion excellent resources out there for that. Do your homework. The greater your knowledge, the greater your chances of success. This book is specifically written to educate you regarding the challenges you will face on your journey to break what's determined to break you. I have found that an ill-prepared generational curse breaker usually becomes a fatigued generational curse breaker before their journey is completed. If that happens, they will either abort the process prematurely or pause so much that it takes them until their life is nearly over to complete the process and reap the benefits of their spiritual labor. No ma'am, and no sir, that CANNOT be your story. Therefore, take a deep breath and make room for Holy Spirit conviction that you can and will win if you faint not!

You've Been Called

So, you've been called to break the bloodline chains and patterns that have been plaguing your family for generations. Congratulations! God sees something in you that can get the job done. Incredible! You should feel elated and elevated. More than likely, you've always felt and even thought differently than most of your family. When you reflect and embrace honesty, you've never truly fit in like everyone else in your family. Either you were treated peculiarly or flat-out rejected. You're not sure why, but thoughts have always demanded that you choose a different path than most of your kinfolk. Maybe you're the only Christian by name and deed. Perhaps you're the only one to regurgitate the bloodline sicknesses while everyone else feasts on them. Whatever differentiates you, you've decided you a different outcome than what your bloodline willingly or ignorantly accepts. You divinely discern that what's going on with your bloodlines is not a natural matter; it's spiritual. And to change it, you're willing to tap into the spirit realm where life-altering orders originate.

You Said, Yes

You eagerly gave God your yes. Good job, but don't get beside yourself. Many are called, but few are chosen (Matthew 22:14). Keeping that scripture in mind, being the designated generational curse breaker doesn't mean that no one else in your family is called to break free. It means that you have what it takes to do it thoroughly should you accept. Just like Joseph and David, you are the MAJOR in the midst of minors. Others in your family may acquire knowledge and put in some work, but when you inspect closer, you will find gaps of inconsistency and sketchy dedication. They don't have what it takes holistically, so God invited you and not them.

Fasten Your Seatbelt

Sorry to burst your generational curse-breaking bubble, but your path to freedom will not be as straightforward or as easy as you may think. Those who have walked ahead counsel you to fasten your seatbelt because saying yes to such a prestigious role can be a tumultuous experience. Your role is not to be taken lightly. The invitation is free. However, you must become spiritually equipped to be chosen and

4

remain relevant during your journey. By the way, my name is Markeida Faithe, and my role as your virtual Power Pusher is to help you fall into the chosen category.

Curse Breaker's Fatigue

You must be vigilant and laser-focused on the assignment to break free. Many faint along the way, but you're guaranteed to win if you faint not (Galatians 6:9). Those who fainted along the way experienced what I have coined as, Generational Curse Breaker's Fatigue. I've found that Generational Curse Breaker's Fatigue occurs because many go into battle unequipped intellectually and spiritually. They are eager and well-meaning but have no idea what is ahead. Some aren't even certain what curses they are fighting. Like you, they see negative patterns that must change and ignorantly dive in. Before you know it, they are diving out, discouraged and fatigued by the blows that come with the assignment. Lift your hands right where you are and resound, *"In the name of Jesus, the Generational Curse Breaker's Fatigue will not be my story. Amen."* If by chance you're already in a state of fatigue, lift your hands and cry out to God, *"In the name of Jesus, revitalize and equip me. Amen.*

Generational Curses

As your virtual Power Pusher, I'm delighted to have your time and attention. It's evident that you are serious about fighting effectively. God has empowered me to help equip and coach his Breakers to success. I will do everything within my power to coach you thoroughly. Before proceeding, let's clarify what a generational curse really is.

A generational curse is a literal curse put on a family by a power of darkness or God (See Appendix A). The curse has negative ramifications that challenge the trajectory of a family's ability to rise in one or several particularly noticeable areas of a family's lineage. Examples of such curses can present in the forms of poverty, marital denial, barrenness, premature deaths, mental illness, chronic rejection, and so on. The curse remains attached to the family until it's challenged and broken by a born-again generational curse breaker like yourself.

The Strongman & Familiar Spirits

The curse is guarded by who the word of God calls, the "strongman" (Matthew 12:29). He is the gatekeeper. He monitors all demonic activity associated with your bloodlines. He determines what powers of darkness can access you and your family. The stipulations of the bloodline curses are recorded and monitored for enforcement throughout the ages by familiar spirits. They are familiar with everyone on the family line and their weaknesses. They are the bloodline record keepers. To successfully dismantle a bloodline curse, you must disempower the strongman and expose and shut down the familiar spirits.

I get frustrated with those who have turned the term *generational curse breaker* into a trendy saying. It's everywhere. What I need you to understand is that you can't ignorantly fall into the cultural hype of shouting that you are a generational curse breaker. Please believe that a generational curse breaker is not just someone who casually changes the negative patterns embedded in a bloodline. The generational curse breaker recognizes negative bloodline patterns and pays the spiritual, emotional, and natural costs to break them.

Breaking the Curse

To break a generational curse, you have first to identify the curse, establish how it got there, track its roots as far back as possible, renounce it, and be prepared to fight the entities that guard it and show up to challenge you. A generational curse is broken ONLY when you break the covenant behind it, not when you merely alter a behavior, wear a t-shirt with the saying, or write it on your social media pages as an impressive affirmation. It's called a curse for a reason.

The enemy is so devious and nasty. He will allow you to think that the curse is broken and watch you stack money, accumulate things, and take them from you when it's too late for you to rebuild. Another game he plays to teach you a lesson is watching your accumulated wealth flow to your children and then cause them to squander it. This is why you must break the curse correctly for lasting generational results.

Resist

Resist comparing your life to that of sinners who are accumulating wealth. They unknowingly and, in some cases, knowingly work for Satan. Their wealth and blessings benefit Satan's kingdom. They or their ancestors paid prices that you know not of. Don't for a moment underestimate how wicked this world is. Don't become distracted or envious of the hype. They will have to give an account on judgment day, just like you and me. Focus and mind 'your' bloodline business.

In the remaining chapters, I would like to share golden truths that no one tells the generational curse breaker at the start of their journey. I am confident that with my insight and your passion for understanding, you will WIN and not faint! However, before you go skipping your excited but exhausted self over to the next page, as your Power Pusher, I believe it's necessary for you to formally accept God's invitation to break bloodline cycles. Pray the following prayer with all of your heart and soul.

Dear Heavenly Father,

Thank you for such a prestigious invitation to be the one to stand up against hindering bloodline curses. I loathe anything with the galls to define how high, wide, and far I and my bloodlines can go. I hereby accept the invitation to take my life back and the wealth of my bloodlines that have been stolen. I submit to the process of becoming equipped. I will not lean on my understanding. Guide me, great Jehovah, and together, we will dismantle the bloodline forces who've forged cracks into my bloodline's foundations. Power must change hands. In the name of Jesus, I declare that what stopped generations before me will not stop me and the generations to come. Amen.

Your Problem Is Spiritual

No one tells the generational curse breaker that wise people do not go into any battle of significance without first studying their opponent and counting the cost (Luke 14:28-30). Breaker, accepting the role of generational curse breaker, is no exception. It would be wise to devote time to becoming well-informed and devising a winning strategy before attacking ancient spirits. Relax and resist rushing and being anxious. Breaking free is a process; if you don't understand that, fatigue will be your portion. Once you start engaging, remember that things stop and reverse in the realm of the spirit before they stop and reverse in the natural. Resist being quick to diagnose that things aren't changing. Your family didn't go under overnight and aren't coming out overnight. However, there is an order you can follow to make things easier. Let's talk about it.

Identify the Curses

So, to win, you must first clearly identify what the bloodline curses are. Look for negative patterns deeply embedded in the bloodline that cause great concern. The patterns should be chronic. For example, it's not a bloodline marital curse if all the women in your family are married and you're not. However, you may have cause for concern if most women in your family can't seem to get married or stay married. Perhaps if they do marry, it's nothing to admire. You're more than likely looking at a bloodline curse if the majority of the bloodline is suffering from chronic poverty or barrenness. Bloodline issues are chronic and present in the majority of the family. Those who are not bloodline breakers may try to remedy bloodline problems carnally. They may even go as far as seeking practitioners of the craft (witchcraft) for assistance or understanding. However, the generational curse breaker discerns that the root of the problem is spiritual and only rectifiable under God's leadership. The generational curse breaker understands that correcting their cracked foundation is the key to advancing in life. Psalm 11:3 asks, "If the foundations are destroyed, what can the righteous do?" Your family bloodlines are your foundations; if they are cracked, whatever you build will fail to prosper.

Center Yourself

Ha! Let me clue you in. All curses are rooted in the spirit and have natural ramifications. Those who aren't bloodline curse breakers are one-dimensional. They don't look deep enough, so their results don't transform generations. Don't get frustrated. You have the Holy Spirit as your helper. He's eager to help you become equipped, so take a deep breath and welcome his guidance. Ask Him to show you the generational curses you're dealing with. Be patient and give Him time to show you. You may have a dream or vision or hear the answer. Tune in. You may already have a knowing embedded within. Either way, be clear regarding what you're aiming to change. If you're warring aimlessly, you will become fatigued, so center yourself and give them the business.

A Life of Holiness

Breaking generational curses is a spiritual act that requires spiritual insight. You can't just jump into the enemy's face without being prepared. That's a quick way to get served. And yes, God will allow it because both kingdoms abide by rules of engagement. Clean up your life. You must deal with your sin before trying to confront the enemy that's been sitting on your bloodline longer than you've been alive. This is where many reject God's offer. They aren't willing to pay the price that being a generational curse breaker demands, and that's holiness. Please grant me time to elaborate further on the importance of living Holy by using a few random examples. Let's say that the generational curse is poverty. You can't successfully challenge poverty while stealing and doing manipulative things. You can't break a marital curse while committing adultery. You can't break the power of rejection with malice and unforgiveness in your heart. Attempting to do so is laughable in the realm of the spirit.

Legal Rights

The state of your soul matters. It matters because the enemy uses your transgressions as an argument to keep his grip secure. Your thievery, adultery, and unforgiveness are legal rights. If you aren't familiar with the term, legal rights, I encourage you to pause your interest in this book and read my book on spiritual warfare, *You Already Know, You Can't Build On A Demonic Foundation.* Learn as much as you can about spiritual warfare before advancing further. However, for those of you who are antsy and impatient and must know now, a legal right is sin that the enemy presents before God as justification to keep you and your bloodlines in bondage.

Curse Cause

You can't ignorantly demand that Satan let your bloodlines go. Think. The word of God states that a curse without a cause cannot stand (Proverbs 26:2). Chile, if it's standing, there's a cause. Let me say it again and differently: if a curse is in place, it got there by some means. The cause and the means are the legal rights. Somebody on your bloodline or someone offended by your bloodline did something to make the enemy believe that he could cage your entire bloodline. You may not know what was done, the Holy Spirit will show you if you ask Him.

Many of you already know the bloodline offenses. You've heard the bloodline chatter. Some of you have had bloodline dreams and visions informing you. Others have heard from God's true prophets the cause. Sometimes, you may have to press the spirit realm for information through prayer and fasting. I also help men and women of God discover such information through my bloodline assessment. Either way, you can get answers if you genuinely want them. Nothing has a right to bring a charge against you without telling you on what grounds! If you apply enough prayer-pressure, dark powers will tell on themselves. Press for understanding and knowledge before fighting, or you will get dealt with and find yourself in the corner, exhausted and mad!

Prayers of Renunciation

One of the main steps is praying prayers of renunciation that are specifically designed to separate you from the dark covenants knowingly and unknowingly made by your ancestors and their enemies. In some cases, praying prayers of renunciation alone will not be enough. You may be among the many confused and tired that your situation isn't changing because you've done all the other steps and prayed countless prayers of renunciation, and nothing is breaking. It may be possible that you have not discovered the true legal right that's holding the bloodline hostage. It could also be that, in your case, you need more aggressive measures such as deliverance, strategic fasting, and incorporating violent warfare prayers at specific times of the night.

When I mentioned deliverance, I meant evicting evil spirits that may have taken up residency within and around you. In such a case, you need a strong and knowledgeable deliverance minister to help expel those spirits. Don't become indignant; we all have spiritual blind spots. Fasting breaks yokes when done correctly. Although popular, I have found that the third watch is not always the proper prayer watch, so make sure you're praying during the correct watch. I know you're thirsting for more in-depth information, but please remember, this book is only designed to inform you of what others haven't told you.

They Are Coming for You

W hat no one tells the generational curse breaker is that dismantling bloodline powers is no easy task. It's not an overnight job. It will take time, consistency, and determination. Breaker, I can't express this point more than I already have. It's a time-consuming process. And when I speak of time, I'm not saying it will take many years. However, it will require time to study and learn how to become equipped in the key areas that the curses stand on. It takes time to learn about dreams, how to war versus pray, how to conduct strategic fasting, and how to recognize the bloodline sicknesses and their roots. You must understand how bloodline spirits retaliate and how to handle those stubborn bloodline problems. Again, you will win if you faint not!

Clap Back, Backlash & Retaliation

I am not excited to share this truth, but here goes, beloved: THEY ARE COMING FOR YOU. You cannot uproot powers of darkness from their home turf and think they will not clap back. You must expect backlash. Hear me and hear me well; the bloodline powers will challenge you. They can't take you out, but they will challenge you and apply pressure to test how serious and robust you are spiritually. They are going to size you up spiritually and fight fire for fire. To shut you down, they will consult familiar spirits to discover your weaknesses and any lingering unaddressed legal rights. They may clap back in your dreams by feeding you, inserting you with a needle, having sex with you, shooting, and chasing you. You may also experience demonic manifestations in the natural. No one told me these things, and I know no one told you, so be prepared. Shut them down before going to bed and upon waking up! And don't allow their stubbornness or threats to coerce you into thinking your actions aren't working. It's a sign that they are. And by the way, canceling a demonic dream is excellent, but the goal is to understand why they're challenging you and go into dismantling mode.

When you go after certain spirits, they will retaliate in the area of their interest. For example, the spirit of poverty may touch your finances to intimidate you. The spirit of sickness and disease may incite a doctor's report from hell! Then what? Will you shut down to hold on to your bread crumbs or stand your ground so you can own the bakery? I'm giving you the truth so that you can adequately prepare.

You Have Help

This is where I call unto your heart that you have help. You have the Most High God and the heavenly host on your side. Take heart! You'll win if you faint not. And because I've been doing this for a long time, I can hear some of you thinking, "If God is on my side, why doesn't He automatically shut them down?" Even chosen generational curse breakers must be tested, tried, and proved. With every battle, you'll grow more robust and more knowledgeable. I believe this is by design so you can reach back and help others through their process. I believe God allows us to go through specific battles not only for our benefit but also for the benefit of those we are assigned to. I can teach you because I've lived through it.

Weapons of Your Warfare

You must develop a lifestyle of prayer and Bible study. There are weapons of warfare that are not carnal but mighty through God for the pulling down of strongholds (2 Corinthians 10:4). Familiarize yourself with the many weapons of warfare so that you can prove yourself to be a worthy opponent against the enemy. And by the way, certain weapons are suitable for certain fights. The Holy Spirit will teach you how to engage and what weapons to use when.

The Important Step

What no one tells the generational curse breaker is that a crucial step to attaining freedom includes engaging in very violent spiritual warfare prayers (during the right Watch) that demand the return of all that was stolen or delayed by the enemy. The violent warfare prayers are designed to weaken demonic forces and pressure them to break their holds. Listen, some go quickly, and others put up a fight intended to wear you out. You are trying to remove them from territory that, yes, belongs to you, but they claim. Remember, there is no cookie-cutter way to win, so working with an equipped spiritual warfare specialist is acceptable if you ever feel stuck.

When you become too hot to handle, the enemy will utilize his famous trick of sending a lukewarm or cold relationship to trip you up. Nothing diverts the generational curse breaker's attention (when they are on the verge of a breakthrough) like a relationship sent from hell. Ponder this: Just because you're chosen doesn't mean you will finish strong. I don't know about you, I must finish strong!

Types of Breakers

No one tells the generational curse breaker that there are two main types of breakers. Type one is called to break free from the bloodline curses. Type two is called to free themselves and lead willing family members to freedom. Breaker, you likely won't know which you are until later in the process.

Be clear. The bloodline's cooperation is needed to enforce a corporate bloodline breakout. You cannot single-handedly break your bloodlines free, which is why scores of generational curse breakers become discouraged, confused, and experience self-condemnation. They expect everyone to follow them. Some would disagree with me, but to me, it's common sense. Think of it this way: the non-breaking of a demonic covenant keeps a curse in place.

Technically, The Bloodline Is Free

There are specific sin offerings that keep curses well-fed. For example, let's say that there is an anti-marital generational curse on your bloodline; once you win the war, all of you are free to go. However, instead of moving forward, cousins Harry, Tony, Todd, Jerry, Skip, and Ralph keep fornicating and practicing adultery. Although, through Christ, you broke the curse, their lives will not reflect such. Their perversion will mature into a revitalized generational curse. However, the curse can no longer touch you. It's impossible to break a godless bloodline free without revival.

The tragedy is that, in many cases, the bloodline never gets the memo that they are free because they are too busy avoiding and talking about you. Most are spiritually blind and fearful of anything that has to do with demons. They only want God in crisis or just enough of Him for relief, void of deliverance. Even so, you will be free. You will be free because you broke the covenant and can enforce your freedom even when the evicted spirits return to reclaim their turf. Makes sense? I sure hope so.

Awesome News

It is possible to be the breaker for only one bloodline. For example, you can be called to break your mother's entire bloodline free while ignored by your father's bloodline. You can break free from both but impact only one on a massive level. You may find it easier to break free from one bloodline over the other. It all depends on how deep the curses run and the depth of the sacrifices used to legitimize the covenants. There is a difference in the weight of a curse fueled by human sacrifices versus chicken sacrifices. Yes, it gets complicated at times, and if you are not well-informed, you will become fatigued while trying to win, so study, study, study.

The fantastic news is that God is sovereign, and your prayers and efforts are robust. There will be relatives whom God chooses at will to prosper, and your bloodline-breaking prayers will grant Him the legal right to bless them despite themselves. They may never come to understand anything about generational curses nor understand that it was you who put in the spiritual work for their freedom where they would have otherwise sat in bondage. In addition, there will be others like yourself (minors) whom God raises to recognize and dislike what the bloodline likes. Their path to freedom will not be as tedious nor challenging because of their obedience and sacrifices.

Blessed Are They

Blessed are the family members who discern and honor the progress of the breaker and come into alignment with them. Blessed are those who work to enforce the breaking of the bloodline curses and the return of everything stolen from them. They will see things improve as they renew their minds and deeds. Pray for revival to hit your family.

Consecration & Isolation

No one tells the generational curse breaker that when God desires to equip them for their assignment, He calls them unto Himself for a season of equipping. This is a truth that many breakers don't understand and try to skip. This is also another reason why many become fatigued. They aren't prepared for the silence and focus that their call requires. Breaker, it's in your place of isolation and consecration God trains you and details your specialty. Yes, you are a generational curse breaker who has an area of specialty. Mine is deliverance and inner therapy. What's yours? If you don't know, you have yet to have your wilderness experience with God.

Before I knew I was the generational curse breaker, I had no idea what was happening within me. I kept feeling the urge to quiet my life and focus on God. I couldn't explain it to others because it was odd and uncomfortable. I felt the pull to steal away, and I obeyed. I now know that God was calling me into a place of consecration by His Spirit. He called me into a year-long consecration, and I was excited. However, when I told those in my circle, some became upset with me. I couldn't understand their attitude. I was stealing away for God's glory, but they either didn't believe me or didn't care. Sects of my family talked about me horribly and started spreading gossip that I had lost my mind. Thankfully, God created me to be quite strong-minded. I didn't care what they thought about my obedience. I surely didn't mind anyone thinking I was becoming a fanatic.

What surprised me most was the jealousy. People around me were jealous of my quiet time with God. I was baffled by their jealousy because God desires quiet time with all His children. Sadly, most put everything before Him. Some people become jealous when they see others in God's lap while they are miles from His feet. However, that is neither your problem nor reason to reject God's invitation to climb to his secret place. If you are genuinely the generational curse breaker for your bloodline, you will receive an invitation to steal away with God. I guarantee it!

During my alone time with him, He purged me of religion and filled me with liberty. We binged on deliverance videos and books. I spent every waking moment not at work studying, praying, and worshipping

God. I utilized all of my extra money to purchase resources and attend deliverance conferences. Coming from a Seventh-Day Adventist background, God had to teach me about the five-fold ministry which included how to engage in spiritual warfare, tap into the prophetic, and utilize my weapons of warfare. He taught me how to identify and solve spiritual problems. And yes, He worked on my heart. Whew! I was such a mess. He was so patient and loving to me. I couldn't get enough of Him. God poured into me much wisdom and knowledge. What an honor it is to be invited to be instructed by God. When my year concluded, I did not want to leave. I loved being in His courts and having Him all to myself. He had to push me back into the world.

I missed family functions, and I didn't date during that time. I dated God. It was in that season that I learned the power behind stealing away. Even now, it's nothing for me to do things by myself. As a matter of fact, because of my training, I live a tranquil life. I crave silence when surrounded by noise for too long. I am rarely in a state where I cannot hear my creator. And no, I'm not weird or socially awkward. I'm beautiful, funny, and very trendy. It's just that I understand my assignment and what it takes for me to always be in position.

Embrace the Invite

Generational curse breaker, embrace the invite to consecrate yourself. It will require that you shut out all unnecessary noise and forfeit all of your extracurricular pleasures for a season. Although God called me into consecration for a year, your time may be shorter or longer. The requirements will vary. If I had to do it all over again, I would not have told anyone what was being requested of me. I brought unnecessary warfare into my time away by communicating what was nobody's business.

Even as I write this book, I'm in a ninety-day consecration with God. I'm behind schedule in completing some personal and ministerial tasks because I allowed myself to become distracted and embraced disobedience. As a result, I almost reached a place of burnout. The people and things I placed before God aren't called to what I'm called to. They can't go where I go in the realm of the spirit. Obedience is better than sacrifice.

Lose Your Mind

Be forewarned that the consecration period is not always comfortable. I distinctly recall feeling like I was going to lose my mind at times when the warfare became extremely thick. This is because I was finally challenging what had been challenging me for many years.

With every prayer prayed and covenant broken, dark powers were throwing darts against my mind and peace. I heard chatter that I should take my life, I was crazy, and I was wasting my time. I didn't know it then, but I was doing severe damage in the realm of the spirit, and those dark entities wanted to shut me down. No one tells the generational curse breaker that things will get extremely wild, and when they do, you're on the brink of a marvelous victory! Don't stop.

Dark Dreams

My dreams got wild. Dark powers came night after night to challenge me. It was surreal. A witch confronted me in one of my dreams, and a spiritual bird attacked me. I awoke to excruciating pain on my left side from the attack. In another dream, a clueless-woman showed up, trying to put a death curse on me. I was mocked by the spirit of Leviathan and attacked by the demonic bae more times than I care to recount. However, I kept going because I knew they could not harm me more than they already had.

Clues

I was a baby, so I didn't realize that they were exposing themselves, and every dream was a clue as to what was fighting me and what I needed to attack. I was in training. As I stated previously, God allowed some things so that I could become equipped to help you. Therefore, accept this advice, and please write down your dreams. You may not understand their meaning, but if you keep studying and ascending higher in God, you will. In my book, You Already Know, I share sixty-three dreams you should not have and how to pray against them.

Watch the Company You Keep

What no one tells the generational curse breaker is to watch whom you give access to. If the enemy cannot get to you directly, he will use those who have access to you to deflate your excitement and drive. They will tell you that it doesn't take all of what you're doing to break free. Stop and think! How would they know what it takes? The enemy will use them to gather information regarding your state of mind, progress, and strategy.

Many generational curse breakers cannot ascend higher because of their mouths. They invite unnecessary warfare into their process all because they have diarrhea of the mouth. They are the main ones suffering from generational spiritual-fatigue spiritual fatigue. They are discouraged and tired from fighting and seeing very little progress. They don't realize that their tongue is their enemy. Generational curse breakers: be wise, quiet, and focused. You are stopping what your parents didn't stop. And if you give up, you will pass the fight on to your children. You must be willing to stand alone when all is said and done.

Natural Works

No one tells the generational curse breaker that they must work both the natural and spirit realms for maximum and lasting results. For example, you may break the spirit of poverty and demand that everything stolen from you be released. However, you still have to attain financial literacy. It's wise to learn how to budget and balance your checking account. Breaker, you are responsible for attaining information to help you develop healthy spending habits and a healthy attitude toward money. You may break the marital curse but must also learn healthy communication skills. You are in charge of how you conduct yourself while dating. You are responsible for who you decide to entertain. You may break the spirit of rejection, but you're still accountable for learning to love and accept yourself.

What I'm communicating may sound like common sense. I'm afraid it isn't for many. Some generational curse breakers became fatigued in the wait because they thought that since they handled things in the realm of the spirit, things would automatically fall into place naturally. This can't happen to you. Warfare does nothing more than clear your path in the realm of the spirit so that you can have clearance to build freely in the natural. You have to put some work behind your faith. You have to work the middle. God may have spoken that you will be a millionaire. The responsible response is to ask Him to order your steps and equip you with winning strategy. You may break the martial curse, you still have to leave the house and meet men. You have to pursue employment. It would be best if you put in the work to heal and combat gluttonous habits. You have to pursue academic greatness. Networking must become a part of your comfort zone. Do you get the point? You have work to do. The excellent part is that you can achieve it all without demonic bloodline interference because you are free.

Family Matters

No one tells the generational curse breaker that they shouldn't waste their time if they are super attached to their family and detaching for a season seems like torture. They may as well tell God that they decline the invite. Breaker, it is impossible to break free from the bloodline holds while attached to those who are bound. Emulate Joseph's example and go ahead of your bloodline to save your bloodline (Genesis 50:20). You must escape from your kindred just as Abraham did (Genesis 12:1). You must see the bigger picture and lead the way.

You can't stay on the level of the curse and break the curse. Think of it this way: the very spirits you are trying to break free from are attached to every person you're tied to. If you genuinely want to help make a difference, ascend higher, break free, and extend a rope to those willing to join you. The delay in separating will undoubtedly lead to fatigue due to the tug of war on the soul. Generational curse breaker, those same family members you're stalling for will be in the same place year after year. This cannot be your portion.

The refusal to separate to elevate has canceled many generational curse breaker invitations. As I stated earlier, many are called, but few are chosen. Unfortunately, this is one of the reasons why. It's a severe offense. Jesus said: "If anyone comes to me and does not hate his own father and mother and wife and children and brothers and sisters, yes, and even his own life, he cannot be my disciple. Whoever does not bear his cross and come after me cannot be my disciple" (Matthew 19:5)

Family Acceptance

What no one tells the generational curse breaker is that their family will not necessarily be happy that God chose them. Some families will be receptive and thankful, while others will not. This is the case if the stronghold of rejection is on the family line. And where rejection resides, jealousy resides with a vengeance. Such bloodlines attack anyone who doesn't share their mentality or seems to be rising above them. In my case, my bloodlines believe to a certain extent but don't want me to be the messenger. Many dislike that God chose me and not them or one of their children. Some wanted my knowledge without acknowledging me. At first, it was hurtful, confusing, and exhausting. I got over it when God taught me that I may be called to the bloodline, but I'm not responsible for the bloodline's reception of me or their freedom.

You Are Not Responsible for Your Bloodlines

You may be called to the bloodlines, but you are not responsible for your bloodlines. All you are requested to do is walk out your freedom and feed those who inquire or are open to learning how to break free. Your light and change of fortune will draw them. Don't force yourself onto anyone. Don't feel pressured to interrupt family events with your new-found freedom and knowledge. You can't make your family see, respect, or hear you. You can't make them put in the work. If you get caught up trying to control their level of reception and activity, you will become tired and discouraged. You will lose ground and any respect that you earned.

You may be the generational curse breaker, but you are not God. And even God respects free will. Give them the respect to choose life or death (Deuteronomy 30:19). Your responsibility is to make sure you are in place to nourish and help educate those who hear and desire differently. And more than likely, they will watch you for a season and, when you least expect it, come to you by night. Don't be insulted by the down-low visitations. Not everyone is as bold and free as you are. Feed them and keep it moving.

Unfortunately, it is probable that initially, your children will not be receptive. You can't control who receives and who doesn't. Please get this deep down in your soul and resist becoming fatigued because you overexert yourself by trying to force truth onto non-receptive hearts. However, be encouraged. Just because they don't have a taste for you this year doesn't mean they won't next year. Some people have to experience the right amount of maturity, loss, and breakdown before they are ready to receive. Resist the urge to be the Holy Spirit junior, and don't take things personally. This is spiritual warfare; you only have one enemy, and his name is Satan. Just live free and allow God to draw all men unto Him (Joh 12:32).

You Are Not Ordinary

No one tells the generational curse breaker that they are not ordinary. Curse Breakers, unless you get this truth through your thick skulls, you will fatigue from trying to convince the world and yourself that you are ordinary. Breaker, God does nothing void of style and class, including choosing his Breakers. No one can tell for sure how He makes the decision. However, I can tell you that He sizes us up, looking for those whose spiritual capacity includes love for Him, endurance, focus, submission, faithfulness, boldness, and obedience. I say this because those are some of the attributes that a generational curse breaker needs for success. With that being said, we just eliminated the majority of the world. Therefore, you are in an elite class. Most people are tossed to and fro by the wind. They may have some discipline regarding natural things but not spiritual things. You must remember that it's not our earthly works that impress God. It's that spiritual stuff that He loves and brags on! He was bragging in Job 1:8, He inquired of Satan, "Have you considered my servant Job?" God knew that Job had fear issues, but He also knew that he had love for Him and sustaining and enduring power. It was during his breaking that he was delivered from anxiety and fear. And for that, he walked away with more than he ever had!

When your eyes become open to the bloodline sicknesses and the causes behind them, you rank up in knowledge. You see and hear differently. With every prayer and resource watched and read, you grow in knowledge and elevate in ways you may not detect. You will see and hear with understanding what others overlook and dismiss. You often speak over their heads, but to you, you sound normal. You will not be invited to casual and carnal gatherings; if you are, the room sighs with relief when you exit. More than likely, you will be the one that others seek for counsel, prayer, and deliverance. Own it and refrain from despising it. You will look and sound foolish trying to fit in where you don't. And you already guessed what I'm about to say; you will become fatigued trying to act ordinary.

If by chance you find a group that desires your company, don't feel ashamed or judgmental if your interest is short-lived, especially when you can't freely talk about your passion. You will eventually become exhausted from being fragmented and distance yourself. You will never have an overflow of friends. Accept it and cherish the very few close friends you do have.

Mixing Friendship & Ministry

What no one tells the generational curse breaker is that although they are not ordinary, they were created to stand out! Breaker, people will be attracted to you because of your God-glow and knowledge. Resist the urge to befriend every excited person who enters your life to feed. They are not your friends. God led them to you to glean and grow. He sent them to you for freedom's sake, not to seek friendship. You will experience disappointment time after time if you don't understand this valuable truth from the jump. You will fatigue and feel used once people copy you, get whatever else they want, and leave. You can avoid disappointment if you understand your role and maintain a professional stance. Like it or not, people don't want you. They want what you know. They want who you are in the spirit. They are drawn to your assignment, and that's how it's supposed to be. Give them what they want with joy and focus, and keep it moving.

I'm not saying that all hearts drawn to you aren't genuine. I'm saying they don't come to you because they need a friend but because they need freedom. When you blur the lines, you will miss crucial freedom moments. Do not allow anyone to cling to you unnaturally and prematurely. This is why it's wise to first heal your abandonment and array of rejection issues before putting yourself out there. Keep ministry as your focus regardless of how wonderful and relatable they are. If you do otherwise, I promise you, things will not end well. They are your assignments and not your friends. I made this mistake many times when I started in ministry and beyond. Learning how to avoid mixing friendship and ministry took me a long time. I have made some beautiful connections, but it was always after my job was done—Ministry over friendship.

Church Jealousy

What no one tells the generational curse breaker is that when they rank higher in knowledge regarding spiritual warfare, they attract warfare from many sides. I talked about family jealousy in a previous chapter. However, there is another area that, depending upon your level of healing, has the potential to hurt and delay you: Church-jealousy. Yes! Breaker, depending upon the depth of your knowledge and call, you will attract jealousy within your ministry. This area almost fatigued me because I was ignorant of how competitive some ministries and church folk can be. Some will:

1. *Attempt to discredit or discount your knowledge.*

2. *Accuse you of being prideful when, truthfully, they feel inadequate.*

3. *Block you from ministering or influencing others with your knowledge.*

4. *Make sly comments that hint at generational curses not being real.*

5. *Compare you to others as if it's a competition.*

6. *Try to privately milk you for information without publicly acknowledging you.*

When God started using me to cast out evil spirits, I requested a meeting with my then-pastor to communicate what was happening in my life; he stood me up. He flat-out avoided meeting with me. It was at that point that I left his ministry. Months later, he sent an email expressing that his church would return to the old ways of incorporating deliverance. For a short while, they started hosting deliverance services. Their efforts eventually fizzled out. They were not equipped to build a lasting deliverance ministry.

As I began to grow and expand in knowledge, many people in ministry came on my Facebook lives to size me up, silently take notes, and act as monitoring spirits. They would never speak or acknowledge that they were there. I attended many conferences where the ministers and pastors wouldn't acknowledge me. Many of those encounters wounded me because I was not healed. In retrospect, they were responding to the dark bloodline rejection assignment resting on my life.

Some Will Try to Use You

When I lived in Alabama, my awakening came when I was contacted by a young woman who was the founder of one of the largest conferences for young women in the area. She was also a church member of the pastor who avoided meeting with me. Although she came by night, I was delighted to hear from her. She communicated that she desired to walk through deliverance and learn as much as possible from me so that she could break free and grow her ministry. She communicated that her ministry was missing deliverance. We exchanged several texts, and I promised to pour everything I knew into her.

During our interactions, the Holy Spirit kept alerting me that her dealings with me were not authentic. I heard Him, but I wasn't so bothered by the truth. I sincerely wanted to see her ministry grow even more, and I did not expect her to share her platform with me. I am blessed and gifted, and jealousy was never a crutch for me, so I didn't mind her motives being skewed. I got the bright idea to invite her to speak at my upcoming deliverance conference. I saw no issue with my request since I was preparing to pour into her. To my surprise, she said she needed to discuss it with her pastor. I chuckled because I knew where this was going. She returned weeks later with a resounding "no," to which I responded, "Not ok, Sis. We have to do better than this." I placed her on block ministry and kept it moving.

I can't tell you the countless ministry visitors who slid into my inbox asking me to promote them without acknowledging me. At one point, a millionaire slid into my inbox, regularly seeking counsel. He was also in ministry and wanted counsel regarding business and personal matters. Everything was great until I asked him to schedule a coaching call. And what do you know, he disappeared quickly.

Sowing & Praying for Access

You will also attract those who try to buy favor with you. They do so by sowing seeds regularly. They want access. They may also try to warm up to you and gain access by telling you they are praying for you or had a dream or vision about you. They may contact you with random prophecies geared toward what you want to hear. Some will profess that they are watching over you and warn against anyone they think is getting too close to you. If you are vulnerable, unhealed, or ignorant of the many devices of the enemy, such occurrences will flatter you and ultimately cause fatigue as python wraps himself around you.

Whether in ministry or not, only some are healed and whole. You must be wise enough to know that not everyone is for you. On the other hand, even if a few try to use you, they aren't necessarily against you. You can't pause after every infringement on your soul to ponder why. People are going to people. Focus and forgive quickly because if you don't, you will become fatigued.

In the beginning stages of my deliverance ministry, I befriended a fellow minister who is now telling her followers that I am a witch. What a despicable fear tactic. I could have easily put this silly woman on blast. However, I chose to forgive her and keep it moving. I could do that because I am an eagle, and my future is lofty. I can't waste time on chicken feed. More importantly, I'm healed, and her silliness couldn't penetrate as it could have in previous seasons. For you see, demonic and soul-wound chatter comes with the territory. Your best defense is to ensure you're healed and be careful to whom you give access. Expect the enemy to use whomever he can for his glory. He's doing his job, so do yours!

Beware of Virtue Drainers

What no one tells the generational curse breaker is that they must be aware of those who come to drain them. Breaker, some people will seek you out because of the anointing on your life. They will spend hours discussing their issues or listening to you pour into them. The unfortunate aspect of this interaction is that they will do nothing with the wisdom and solutions you share. They will seek you out as often as you are willing to entertain them. To your disgust, you will see no application or progression in their lives.

Fatigue can set in because you released spiritual energy into poor soil. These individuals are not seeking change. They are seeking attention. And yes, I understand that one man plants, one man waters, and the other reaps. However, how many times will you plant the SAME crop in the SAME field? If they allow the seeds to die, progress will never occur. Furthermore, such people have several people that they dump on. You are one of many who they cycle through. They are virtue drainers

Don't allow anyone to prostitute your anointing. Be Holy Spirit led in all things. Fruitless banter is kryptonite to a generational curse breaker. Don't allow your unhealed sound wounds to cause you to entertain the SAME dialogue cycle after cycle. If you can't save your bloodline, you can't save a wandering Christian. Setting limits with your time, money, and anointing is okay. You are in control of establishing healthy boundaries against virtue drainers.

Finish Your Process

No one tells the generational curse breaker that they should finish their process first. Breaker, lend me your ear! Avoid the fatiguing and sometimes fatal mistake of trying to save others without finishing your process. Nothing is worse than a half-baked generational curse breaker trying to save others. WOW! Submit to God and allow Him to release you when He's ready. Don't do more or less than what He instructs you to do. There are levels to this thing, and if you get ahead of God, you will be sorry. Pace yourself and be anxious for no platform or to be heard. I desire that I could do some things over. I would decline every conference I was invited to speak at. None of them were suitable for me. I wanted experience, and I was eager to be used by God. None of those platforms improved my life or ministry. I needed time to find my ministry niche.

A Set Time

In one of the previous chapters, I wrote about the rejection accompanying ministry, but that's not everyone's experience. Sometimes, the anointing on your life will draw overwhelming acceptance. That's wonderful. However, resist being propelled into ministry too early. Just because you're gifted and knowledgeable doesn't mean it's your time to be openly used by God. Although Jesus was the son of God, He had a set time to be propelled from obscurity to notoriety. God's time is the best; you will recognize the shifts if you are spiritually woke. Also, be careful not to accept ministerial roles and assignments beyond the scope of your call and knowledge. Sometimes, people will give you the superwoman cape. If you genuinely desire to rise, find your spiritual niche and become an expert.

Minister to Your Soul

Although called by God, you are human, with human experiences and emotions. While you're breaking curses, don't forget to minister to your soul. All the rejection, abandonment, shame, and dishonor you experience throughout your lifetime needs to be ministered to. Your wounded inner prince/princess must be parked so the King/Queen in you can rise and enjoy the fruit of your labor. Nothing is wrong with being broken; however, there is something wrong with remaining broken. You may be very effective in ministry but if your soul issues aren't attended to, you will cause unnecessary damage and attract needless warfare. Whew! Ask me how I know! If you need inner healing, *grab* my four-part book series, *Love On Your Rank In God.*

Finish Your Process

Finish your warfare before trying to deliver/teach your family and friends. If you don't, you will attract unnecessary attacks upon your life. The enemy will lay you out because you're out of order and ministering prematurely. Relax. You will have your time to shine. Ensure that it's when you have put in the work to the point where the enemy hates seeing you rise in the mornings. Finish your process to the point where your name is on hell's hit list. Finish your process to the point where you see the one-hundred-and-eighty-degree turn in your life. Finish your process to the point where you're mature in the things of God and the ways of people so that you avoid tearing things up. Otherwise, you already know, fatigue will be your portion.

Have Fun

No one tells the generational curse breaker that they will become fatigued if they become so heavenly-minded until they're no earthly good. Breaker, you don't have to be stuck up or so uptight that you can't relax and have fun. Stop being so serious. It doesn't make you holier than others! It's ok to relax and enjoy life. You have personality and a unique sense of being. Your uniqueness is designed to help attract those assigned to you by God. You can't stay in fight mode 24/7. You have to discern when to rest and let your hair down. It's ok to laugh, travel, and dance to beautiful music. If you are married, have plenty of sex and date nights. While modesty is the standard, you don't have to dress like the Virgin Mary. Embrace color. Be eclectic! You don't have to adopt a bland life to announce that you are the generational curse breaker.

Liberty in Your Role

You mustn't see the world as your enemy. Just because you are the generational curse breaker doesn't mean you are better than your family and friends. Respect them and resist the urge to call out their dysfunction constantly. You want to draw them and not repel them. No one wants to follow a sour-puss generational curse breaker. There is liberty in your role, so make it work for you! Enjoy yourself when you are around your family and the atmosphere is pleasant enough to thrive, smile, and laugh. If, by chance, the atmosphere shifts, politely excuse yourself without making a scene. You don't have to say a word. Even if they talk about you, they may not admit it, but they will know why you excused yourself.

Adopt hobbies and do things that make you feel alive. I enjoy looking at houses, refinishing furniture, decorating, and watching movies from early settlement periods. I enjoy dancing and listening to the Blues. I find enjoyment in healthy cooking and exercising. I find politics interesting, and I enjoy traveling. When I teach healing and warfare classes, I include humor and am not afraid to show my humanity. This makes me relatable and helps others know that if I can, so can they. Generational curse breaker: you are not a robot. You are alive, so act like it.

Rest

If you are in ministry, listen to your body and rest when it needs a break. When I'm in relaxation mode, I avoid ministering and don't allow people to pull me out of that place. I decline sitting around the pool on a beautiful Saturday afternoon discussing demons. Nope! It's not going to happen. It's your responsibility to do what is required to ensure that you not only avoid becoming fatigued but disgruntled because you feel like you're missing out on life. Generational curse breakers are allowed to have fun!

Attracting Kingdom Love

No one tells the generational curse breaker that if they take the role seriously, answering the call of generational curse breaker will make it more challenging to attract a kingdom mate, especially if they're battling a marital generational curse. Breaker, men/women will flock to you, thinking they are romantically attracted to you. And if you are desperate to be found or naive, you will believe them without discerning that your light drew them. You must be patient and discerning and inquire, *Who sent you*? When you are engaging a person who is attracted to your light and not you, when you show any humanity, they can't handle it. They are attracted to the superman/superwoman in you. They aren't checking for the total essence of who you are. So please utilize wisdom so that you can stop falling for assignments.

Relational Rejection

Accept it. You will experience a lot of rejection. You must understand that multitudes of Christians are merely playing church. They aren't concerned with selling out for God. Your focus will be a turnoff to the wrong man/woman. This is also because the generational curse breaker is set apart and attracts a lot of warfare. The wrong love alliance can be a great distraction and damage your destiny by ushering in setbacks and perimeters that stress your ability to rise. Instead of supporting and covering you, they will become jealous of you and fight your peace in various ways. You will find yourself sleeping with the enemy! The generational curse breaker does not have time to marry the enemy to their destiny. They can't run the risk of fighting bloodline powers and their mate. In addition, they shouldn't be expected to fight their bloodline and their mate's bloodline alone. Their mate must walk with a suitable level of understanding regarding spiritual warfare and maturity.

The generational curse breaker can quickly become fatigued fighting the person who should be fighting with them. Such a mate must be sought through prayer, fasting, and patience. Leaning on your strength and taking all relationship rejection personally will lead to fatigue. You don't have time for that type of distraction. There is a suitable mate for you, and God is the most excellent matchmaker

EVER! Even so, when the right one walks into your life, the enemy will fight you with every fiber of his being. Two generational curse breakers coming together as one is dangerous and a significant bloodline curse-breaking threat. However, what can he do with two people in love and on fire for God and their bloodlines?

Fighting in Your Strength

No one tells the generational curse breaker that they're headed straight for fatigue when they forget who called them and is empowering them to fight. Breaker, it's so easy to get beside yourself, especially when achieving spiritual victories. Resist leaning to your understanding and allow God to lead you every step of the way. As I mentioned earlier, do not stay in fight mode 24/7. You must know when it's time to fight and when it's time to rest. Make the Holy Spirit your best friend. Lean on Him for instructions. When you don't have answers, don't guess. Humble yourself and ask for guidance. Don't try to war or counsel in areas that are beyond your scope of knowledge or elevation.

Remain a forever student under the leadership of God. Resist trying to find covering on your own. Allow God to be your covering until He specifically places you under the leadership of another. I made several people upset because I refused to allow them to choose me without me choosing them. And some leaders rejected my request for their covering. When the connection is proper, you will know, and heaven will smile. Remain submitted to God, and He will strengthen and exalt you past your wildest dreams.

Breaker's Remorse

No one tells the generational curse breaker that there is such a thing as generational curse breaker's remorse. Breaker, this is the chapter that I want you to read and digest very slowly. Generational curse breaker's remorse is when you feel guilty for leaving your family behind in your quest for higher and more significance. Generational curse breakers have beautiful hearts. They want everyone to get it. They want everyone to win. Unfortunately, not everyone will get it or win.

Generational curse breaker, it is normal to feel remorse as you begin to live and think higher than those you left behind. You may find yourself hiding your blessings and downplaying them. Neither pleases God. And no, I'm not encouraging you to be flashy or prideful. I'm encouraging you to give honor where honor is due. I'm encouraging you to live free. You cannot put a muzzle on your gratitude. You were obedient. You put in the work. Generational curse breakers are generational blessing recipients. Your life is supposed to change for the better. Prosperity of the soul and spirit follows deliverance. And when the soul and spirit prosper, blessings are attracted to you.

People in your family will put their mouths on you no matter what. Expect it and forgive them. They are not free. They laughed at how you were struggling while professing God's goodness. And now they are yapping after the goodness of God has shown up. So what! It comes with the generational curse breaker's territory. Let them talk. Do you want to trade places with them? Of course not, so lift your head and give all glory to God. And when someone says to you, "Hmm, it must be nice," respond confidently, "It truly is."

Inner Child Fear

Resist the pull of your inner child, who may fear rejection or being alone. You may have to minister to her fear of prosperity because lack is all she knows. Give her permission to prosper, relax, and enjoy the blessings of God. Reassure her that the blessings are permanent. This may be hard for her if she's accustomed to cycles of rising and falling.

Reject Egypt

Reject the pull to return to Egypt because of the pressure to simulate. Do you know how sick this world is? Plenty of people would love to have you in their lives. So before you return to the pigpen, ask God to give you a new family. That's what I did, and He answered. And for those of you who feel some sense of financial obligation to your family, I understand. This is the case for a lot of cultures. I will not advise you to turn your back on those who depend upon you. However, I encourage you to set healthy boundaries and utilize wisdom. It's one thing to care for mom, but it's another kind of animal to care for her while she's practicing witchcraft. You're giving into the debilitation of your foundation. It's another kind of animal when she's degrading and debasing you. There is danger and dishonor there. Those are cases where you must implement tough love.

Lastly, it's ok to grieve those you left behind, but you can't remain stuck grieving. We've all been given free will. Many of your family members are squandering their lives away, and watching their spiritual downfall hurts. I get it. Pray for them as you move forward. Don't dim your light; brighten your light. Someone in the family will be inspired by you even if they don't tell you. You are breaking bloodline limitations and exposing them to a new standard. Growing up, not going to college was a non-negotiable. It was my bloodline standard. I didn't witness my parents do it. However, I saw other family members do it. Someone eventually paid the price to defy the educational line of demarcation, and I thank them. Generational curse breaker, keep rising because I promise you, someone is watching, and they are rising with you.

Good News

Well, we've come to the end of our road together. I pray this book has been a major blessing to you. It's always good to end things on a high note when possible, so here goes! No one clarifies to the bloodline breaker that they are the bloodline blessing recipient. Breaker, when you break bloodline curses, you have the right to go into the enemy's camp and take back what he stole not only from you but also from your ancestors. The enemy has claimed every released blessing that they died without getting. When you enter his kingdom, you have a right to demand that those things be released and flow into your hands. And THAT, my loves, is good news!

You may have started this book feeling fatigued. Prayerfully, you now feel energized and encouraged. Step away from the battle long enough to reflect, recharge, and strategize. Just don't quit. Heaven and your family (even if they don't know it) are counting on you. You will win if you don't faint!

Appendix A

Genesis 3:14, Genesis 3:17, Genesis 5:29, Genesis 8:21, Genesis 12:3, Proverbs 3:33, Proverbs 22:14, Malachi 2:2, Isaiah 24:6, Lamentations 3:65, Malachi 1:14, Malachi 4:6, Hebrews 6:8, Romans 9:3, Matthew 25:41, Deuteronomy 28:16-19

The Power Pusher invites you to connect with her on her Facebook, Twitter, and Instagram accounts. For more information regarding upcoming classes, private services, and ministry invites, please visit, The Power Pusher's website: www.thepowerpusher.org

www.ingramcontent.com/pod-product-compliance
Lightning Source LLC
LaVergne TN
LVHW051159080426
835508LV00021B/2714